M000295341

EPIPHANIES

Kim Bridgford

EPIPHANIES

David Robert Books

© Kim Bridgford 2013

David Robert Books
P. O. Box 541106
Cincinnati, OH 45254-1106

Design: Pete Duval
Author photo: Marion Ettlinger

ISBN: 9781625490193
LCCN: 2013936268

For Pete and Nick

ACKNOWLEDGMENTS

Able Muse: "That Stillness" (fifth section)

The Chaffin Journal: "Mind and Body" (second section)

The Christian Century: "Doubting Thomas," "Jacob's Ladder"

Christianity and Literature: "Salt Formations"

Commonweal: "That Stillness" (first two sections)

Conversations on Jesuit Higher Education: "Jesus Walking on Water," "Judas"

Cortland Review: "The Carpenter," "The Tree of Life"

Evansville Review: "The Tree of Knowledge"

The Iowa Review: "Offerings"

Measure: "Solomon's Test"

New Zoo Poetry Review: "Joseph and the Coat of Many Colors"

North American Review: "Satan Presents His Side of the Case"

The Penwood Review: "Mind and Body" (first section)

Poem: "The Birth of Jesus" (second section)

String Poet: "Cain and Abel"

Time of Singing: "Mary Magdalene," "Noah"

Umbrella: "That Stillness" (third section)

Westview: "Moses in the Bulrushes"

***

"Offerings" appeared in my collection *Instead of Maps*, published by David Robert Books, 2005.

"Salt Formations" appeared in *Imago Dei: Poems from Christianity and Literature*, edited by Jill Pelaez Baumgartner, 2012.

"That Stillness" (first two sections) received second place for best original poetry from the Catholic

Press Association of the United States and Canada. "That Stillness" (third section) was nominated for a Pushcart Prize.

I am grateful to the Ignatian Residential College at Fairfield University, which provided financial support of this book. I am particularly grateful to Nancy Dallavalle.

TABLE OF CONTENTS

Now we see but a poor reflection in a mirror; then we shall see face to face. Now I know in part; then I shall know fully, even as I am fully known.

1 Corinthians 13:12

OLD TESTAMENT

Satan Presents His Side of the Case

You push and push, and then it doesn't matter,
For once you've pushed beyond what you have said,
You can't go back. You might as well be dead.
And that's where I will start: with myths to shatter.

If He had said, I think you have some gumption,
Instead of pulling out the battle in the air;
If He had said, I made the wrong presumption,
Let's talk about it; let's do what seems fair,

I might have fallen back to peaceful ends:
An angel who, with admiration, tried
To emulate and fill my soul with pride.
I like to think I would have listened then.
I like to think we would have battled sin.
I like to think that we could have been friends.

The Tree of Knowledge

The commandment was to leave my fruit alone—
The apple with the taste of the horizon—
And, as the tree that bore this fruit, I knew
The burden that it carried. Angels passed,
Their evanescence casual, yet Eve—
And Adam too—were drawn to that lost taste.
I wished I could have said to walk away;
I wished I could have said to hesitate.
Yet, in that backyard paradise, my fate
Was to stand while the wind would linger and then leave
Its coolness on my leaf-tips and my view.
I call such lightness faith. That's what I say
In answer to the rot of earth's debris.
They didn't want to end up just like me.

The Tree of Life

They didn't eat of me. They ate the fruit
That dangled with a snake made resolute
To tempt the world. They didn't eat of me.
Yet I would offer immortality.

It's shocking. Such a preferable choice,
And yet they listened to a writhing voice.
For once you eat of me you'll be like God.
I taste just like the lining of a cloud,
And like the sun, and like the shining planets.

The angels feast with airy smiles, for it's
Their life: all recognition recognized,
And all things holy now made undisguised.

The only thing I cannot do is die.
I'm told it tastes like ash, or a good-bye.

Cain and Abel

Abel

When I praise God, I offer Him what's best:
The answer to the glory of His will.
He made me so I'd yearn to pass His test,
And bow my head to the invisible.

And this is good, and thus I too am good.
How else but know these things? How else but see
That I live here because God says I should?
I get my value from His faith in me.

When I speak thus, Cain doesn't like my talk.
He likes to question everything: as if
To do so is what makes a human life.
Do I do everything for God's own sake?
Yes, I say, *yes*. I gather up my song
That serves as prayer, and proves my brother wrong.

Cain

And when I open my eyes, I love the earth.
I love the trees, the sky, the stars, the air.
It seems that I remember my own birth,
The way I knew already how I'd tear

Into existence, make a place for who
I was. Yet Abel doesn't value choice;
If God's the sound, then Abel is the echo.
I told him that he has to have a voice

To realize himself. Why was he made?
What makes him different from a hill or tree?
Why can't he see the world and be like me?
Yet he cannot. He's on the side of God,
The way a shadow trails behind the light.
To live, I have to understand what's right.

Abel

If I am chosen over Cain, my brother,
If the way I represent myself is held in
More esteem; if I am favored by my Father,
If Cain calls out, but never is called in,

What's that to me? I am superior.
Listening to God, I find that Cain is weak,
His mind erected as a barrier
Between what's selfish and what is at stake.

I cannot help but say that he is lost.
I'm pure as clouds, and speak with God's own blessing.
He speaks as what? Himself? What is the cost?
To be the one in whom something is missing.
He tells me that's not true, explains his thirst.
I tell him I improve what was made first.

Cain

He looks at me; his eyes are like a knife.
No one can see the evil there in him.
You cannot spit on someone else's life.
You cannot be so cold, or speak in dim

And abstract ways. In blood I feel such shame.
How can this distant voice be my own brother?
How can we be so different yet the same?
When I see him, it's like I see the weather:

A force that happens, nothing that is kin.
Yet he is chosen, when he is much less.
I am rejected, because I am not he.
I cannot give another offering when
The cost of it would leave me standing, speechless.
How can a man obey and still be free?

Abel

If I'd been told my body would be open
To the air, it's true I would have been surprised.
God didn't tell me anything would happen;
God didn't tell me that I'd soon be eased

From this life. Now I understand what Cain
Once said about the beauty of the earth.
Look at my flesh: a miracle of pain
And joy, the mysteries of death and birth.

If I could thank Cain now I would, for I
Would tell him now I know just what he said.
I miss the touch of earth beneath my feet.
I'm part of God, yet soul without a body
Is cold. The who-I-was in Abel's dead.
I'm floating, loose, within the infinite.

Cain

I thought that, once he died, I could go on.
And yet I find that everything's the same.
Each day there's light and dark; each day the sun
Rises and falls, and speaks my brother's name.

My guilt has changed the face of everything.
He didn't know himself, but God made him
The way that he made me. That one fact stung
The two of us. Now blood itself has come

To take the place of all our violent words.
I loved my brother, though he was a stone.
I loved him, though we were two different men.
One simple issue broke us into shards:
To question or obey? I know the cost
When all of love's vast argument is lost.

Noah

You lived out in the middle of a desert,
And suddenly you heard a voice that said,
"You need to build an ark." And so you did.
Each day you worked. They laughed. You played the part

Of fool that hears vague somethings in the wind.
When asked why you had built the boat so big,
You said it was for animals to stand
With ease. Each elephant, and snake, and dog

Would have a place. They laughed so hard they cried.
Yet later, when the water came, they begged;
They clawed the outer rim of what you made.
What could you do? Their voices weakened, gurgled,
And stopped. You lived inside poetic vision,
A world you'd made beyond all human reason.

Salt Formations

Lot's Wife

I turned and looked when told that I should not,
And turned to salt, a statue of a woman.
And yet it was my tears that made me human.
Who doesn't say good-bye? If this is sin,

I stand as sin; if what I did was wrong,
I stand as emblem of that human failing.
Our tears are present underneath each song.
They speak our joy, and hurry up our healing.

I'll be a blessed warning to you all.
I didn't listen, and had to look again.
Because I'm human I am vulnerable
To thinking of the person I have been.
If you should travel by me, do not wince.
You'll find the taste of your experience.

Firstborn Daughter

I won't cry anymore. What is the use?
We're living in this cave with Lot, our father,
And all he talks about is how he is
The one who got away. He mourns our mother,

Yet is more interested in each scheme
That turns each day to nothing. Now his age
Confuses what God once passed down to him.
Off by himself, he will repeat each message.

I've had enough of what's lost in the past.
I want a present moment that will last
Into the future. Then, one day, I know
That I will lie with him, that I will go
And make him drunk, so he won't see. I am
The one who takes the moment back from him.

The Younger Daughter

I saw what she had done, and did the same,
So I could have a future to my name.
I held him, in a bundle, to my breast,
And felt I'd gathered back what I had lost.

And I thought, *Mother. This* is who I was,
And who my mother was, as she stood there,
Looking for the history in the pause
Between the steps of people and the air.

For people are not human without loss
And joy, the two emotions of our lives.
She knew, without the past, she would be less.
Yet we can also rewrite narratives.
It's both of these I'll pass on to my son.
He'll recognize the meaning of a woman.

Sarah

I.

He told me how the quiet words had come
About necessity of sacrifice,
That Isaac was to lie down for that voice,
And die. The knife was there for Abraham.

It was a test. But we replayed that day.
What if our lives had gone the other way?
We loved our son; through him our world was whole.
Each day we felt a withering of soul.

It is unnatural for children to
Lie down before their parents like a lamb.
The world was different; we saw all through him.
Each moment hung with what we had been through.
We would, in time, become the metaphor
For measuring one's love, and who loves more.

II.

And only later when God gave his son
Did we conceive our human practice run,
How difficult to make the sacrifice.
Yet while the two of us would second guess,

The Lord did not. His son would walk as human,
Would travel down the birth canal of woman,
And feel the dust and murmurs in his heart.
Until the very end, he played his part.

While Isaac was released, God's son would die.
He didn't understand, yet would comply
The way obedience does, when it is good.
He did what God the Father said he should.
He illustrated, when we think it's over,
Love, leaning down, will slit the jugular.

Moses in the Bulrushes

Inside a little basket, down he sailed,
A mother's boat of love and desperate wishes,
And there was Moses, caught within the bulrushes.

How many mothers, knowing death was ruled,
Chose methods such as this, and hoped for good,
A baby on church steps, like wrapped-up food,
Or tangled in the garbage with a note,
Or in despair would slit their baby's throat?

And as happens in the best of literature,
The nursemaid that was chosen was his mother,
And through initial loss he found his nature.
When other mothers leave, and it goes wrong,
Have pity for the faith within their song.
They took this way because they saw no other.

Joseph and the Coat of Many Colors

He wore a rainbow wrapped within his coat.
His brothers' jealousy wrapped around his throat,
And theirs. Because their father wept to hold him,
They banded all together, and they sold him.

And he went on to lead a different life,
The way unwanted children take their grief
And change it into something else. But like
The rainbow, he transformed the storm and ache

And brought about a prophecy for the sake
Of his people. He read dreams, and second to the Pharaoh,
He showed that he knew just the way to share a
Vision that was woven, but oblique.

His father knew that Joseph would inherit,
But was it fair that he announce his favorite?

Jacob's Ladder

At first, I saw their faces, close together,
And in their distance they were like the weather,
The satisfaction found in abstract thought,
The feeling of the sunlight when it's caught.

Then they moved closer, barefoot on the ladder,
And less transparent as they moved toward matter.
And so it was that they became more human,
Their otherness unfolded to illumine

How I could be. Inside my human body,
I tried to understand, but was not ready.
I slept. I watched the swaying of the rungs,
Heard whispering of nighttime on their tongues—

Then nothing but the planets in their voices.
The space they left was filled with human choices.

Solomon's Test

A mother would not cut her child in two.
She'd rather have another woman
Raise her son; yes, she would rather let him go.

And if this were to pass, she'd stand, mouth open—
Grief and garments billowy and wild—
Dust in her mouth, and eyes, and throat. She grieves
The blade before it falls, before the child

Is lopped in two. And she who agrees to halves—
Half love, half-truths, half measures, half a skin—
Might as well have been born another creature, a stone
Or tree, a lacy filigree of mosses.
A mother doesn't trade her dead son in,
Agree to watch the knife-blade enter skin.
A mother doesn't calculate her losses.

Job

I understand you now, Job. *Good* has nothing
To do with it, but *God* does. In the end, it's what
Troubled you late at night, while you lay, mouthing
Your stunted, wishbone prayers. You were all set,

Weren't you? You followed all the rules. And still,
The others who did less and envied you—
You who did *everything* that was asked of you—
They ended up in better places, with it all.

You did the most, and you received the least.
You were the kindest, and there was a cost,
As if the price for excellence were *you*.
And you paid it: once, twice, three times. Meanwhile,
The others felt a secret kind of smile.
Of course, it was wrong. But that's what people do.

NEW TESTAMENT

The Birth of Jesus

Jesus

You were the light around which people gathered.
The stable smelled of animals and blood.
The journey here was hard, and it was good,
The way that kings and wisdom both had weathered

To share, in search of holiness, a room.
How was it when they leaned down toward your face?
Did you see in that ordinary place,
The way you would, when hanging from your doom,

The sense of how a moment's pause could tip?
What did you know, or could you even see—
And in that sense were you like any baby—
Or were you like a seer or a map

That knew itself, a flesh and sky connection
Through blood and stone and cries of resurrection?

Mary

The dark was verging into blue, like water,
And the opening around me was opaque,
Like water, and the moment had the ache
Of waiting, turning into what is better.
I turned his body to me with a kiss,
And knew this was the nature of God's business.
I blinked: I saw him die, and live again.

The animals, made close and warm with breath,
Stood next to us. The stars removed their distance.
Then kings leaned down, their narrow faces awed.
They saw, I think, the blood, and cross, and death.
They saw a child, the one to bring us sustenance.
It smelled like animals in there, and God,
And hope, like water. He's not *if* but *when*.

The Carpenter

To be raised by one who built things was a gift.
To be raised by one who saw that out of air
A room was made, or pieces of a chair.
The world was known by measurement and heft.

As he grew up, he learned the way to touch,
As if the world held secrets in its clutch,
Which he would then reveal. He grew to see
That in the commonplace there's mystery.

A tree would speak of unbuilt shapes within it
The way that Jesus knew the infinite.
He worked in words, and handled them like wood,
Creating lasting work that he called good.

He shaped the clouds into his father's face
For those who had before seen only space.

Mind and Body

Variations on the word *platter*

John the Baptist

I baptized Jesus Christ in holy water.
I told him that he was, in truth, the better
And should have baptized me. He said the letter
Of the Word must be as written, like a ladder

Down from heaven to the earth. Much later
I would meditate on this, how bitter
He could have been, to yield himself to greater
Powers than his own. He trusted his creator.

And when I was imprisoned, Herod's daughter,
To prove a point, asked only that he let her
Exact as payment—and he would not upset her—
My severed head upon a silver platter.

What did it mean? Just flesh and blood to feed her.
And I would learn how mind wins over matter.

Herod

She knew that what she wanted I would get her,
That I was powerless. I was afraid her
Eyes would read the truth of mine, the ardor
That shouldn't grace a father or a leader.

The words were said. I knew it was his head or
Nothing, the way a proclamation's wrought: for
Good or bad. Yet this request had made her
The ruler of desire, the true insider,

The hand that took the hand of what would aid her
And kissed its palm. I wish that I could read her
Mind, that she had danced for me. O writer
Of my destiny, O sweet debilitator

Of my will. Perhaps he died because of fate or
Because I had to show her that I need her.

Offerings

Mary

What does God-sex feel like? Is it the thrill
Of looking at the sun, or the slow tremor
That shakes the body like a miracle?
Is it the arrow piercing through the armor?

Or is it nothing but the feeling that
Something new is just about to happen:
A flower unfurling, the shaping of a thought,
The idea of an apple made to ripen?

The impossible for you was like a cup
You drank from, and you, in turn, believed
That when you suffered you were lifted up
And when you trusted you were also loved.
Like any mother, you were filled with hope,
The world now just the husk where he arrived.

Joseph

You loved her, and it didn't matter what
The others said. You knew what she'd been through,
And if the story strained, you said, "Tell it
Again." And she did until she saw the world in you.
That kind of love is called a miracle.
At night you curled into each other's hips,
But sometimes you would think how she would call
The sunrise God, the dazzle made of shapes
That otherwise would merely hold a space.
So what. You'd be the shadow to that sun;
You'd be the father to her quickened child.
If on the changing sky, she saw His face,
You thought that she'd forget. "Our child is the one."
"Our," she said. "Our." And you were reconciled.

Jesus

It's the only family that I ever knew,
And I loved them. Yet poets always know
They're born to live another kind of life:
The hyperbolic dailiness of grief.
I looked: I saw the homeless and the sick.
I listened to the ordinary music
Of prayer, of wind like breath along the sand,
And in them felt both oracle and end.

And when He spoke to me, I called him Father.
He was my Muse, this iridescent Other,
His knowledge rubbed like oil against my skin.
He opened up my spirit, like the weather,
And when I spoke, we made the poems together.
He said I'd live forever, till I'd listen.

God

I am so perfect, sitting in the skies.
To prove that I would gladly sacrifice
Through blood, who am immortal and alive,
I'll offer up my son. That way I'll grieve
The way that humans understand: to lose
What matters most, the thing they'd never choose.
I'll choose it; I am perfect, being God.
My son is the embodiment of good.
I will not hold him yet. He'll have a woman
On the earth to raise him into what is human,
And later he will meet me on a cloud
And tell me what it was to be allowed
To walk upon the earth, with bitterness,
And know the thorns that I could only guess.

Jesus Walking on Water

The water was belief he walked upon.
The water was a boat that he was on.
The water wrapped their awe up in its smile.
The water was a simple miracle.

Sometimes there had to be a show of power
To illustrate where earth and heaven blur,
Where expectation doesn't meet the eyes,
And loaves and fishes will materialize.

Like Peter who would walk beside him there,
Sometimes we need the way to put our bare
And trepidatious feet upon the lack
Of solid ground, and feel the shifting magic
Of stars that take their time to throw their light
While faith is sturdy with the infinite.

Mary Magdalene

He gathered all around him those for whom
Society would make but little room:
The lepers, poets, prostitutes, and mad,
The true believers, and the truly sad.

And he said, *These are all my people. These.*
It was as if he saw beneath our skin,
And when he asked if he could enter in,
It was a pleasure just to answer yes.

I kissed his feet, anointed him with hair,
And loved the words with which he loved the air.
The day they stood around me, all in stone,
I felt the weight of being all alone,
And he made otherwise what would have been:
I still can taste the blood as they moved in.

The Transfiguration of Jesus

And on the mountaintop he turned to white,
And talked to those that were already gone.
It was as if he were not really human
Or human made into a piece of light.

Who can forsake the flesh in just this way?
Who can, in yearning, show he is an angel?
By doing this, he showed another angle,
Just as a gifted teacher an convey

Another level of his countenance.
We knew the inner speech of radiance.
Yet then he was returned, as flesh, to us.
It's easier, sometimes, to turn to business

And to remember, in the dark alone,
The way he was beyond all flesh and bone.

The Last Supper

He said, *Here is my body and my blood.*
We ate from him, and then we called it good.
We ate his words, and miracles, and hope.
Why not the man in human envelope?

(And in the mystery of communion later,
He'd take the place of wine and also bread.
The taste of God was on their tongue—both red
And white, like familiar words from a love letter,

Revealing all the passion of the text.)
The feeling of our holiness came next,
And how he'd give us everything, and this,
Which was amazing sacrifice to us,

Was just another form of illustration.
When we were hungry, he would be a ration.

Judas

I sold my Lord for thirty coins of silver;
I sold my Lord the way that he had said.
According to the prophecy, he's dead.
I am the one to blame, the one to pilfer

The dirty skirts of history, and to find
That I am now a scourge to all mankind.
My name is but a synonym for how
You do not treat a loved one, like a crow

That feeds upon misfortune, in the flesh.
And it is this, I think, that made me wash
My hands of life. I couldn't stand the grief
That rippled into years with no relief.
I like to think I saw him in the noose
That kicked the world away and cut me loose.

At the Tomb

And he was gone: the body which we ate.
And he was gone: the body on the cross.
Instead, the gaping mouth of nothingness.
And in that moment, we would hesitate,
Because when looking at a miracle,
However much you understand, you don't.
And then I knew: that God from heaven sent
A message to transcend the physical,
The way that words, in all their rawness, burn
When they are real; the way we know a kiss;
The way we watched the blood drip from the cross.
I stood inside that moment and would learn
That I must re-imagine what was known.
I closed my eyes, and saw him rise through stone.

Doubting Thomas

I wish that everything could be like this—
Sex, for instance. Love. To touch the blood
Of someone else by reaching deep is kiss
Made holier than kiss, by Jesus made

Into the resurrection of the body,
And by the God for Whom he is the son.
I feel that I was born to do this duty,
To place my hand inside of such a one

And gasp. I am the awe of the beloved,
Who finds fulfillment in the commonplace,
The one who hears the footsteps, sees the face,
And weeps. True, some by their belief are moved.
Not me. His blood is drying on my fingers.
The scent of who he is, and was, still lingers.

That Stillness

Lazarus

How to explain what I do not remember?
For though my body was undone in death,
My spirit was there, like a holy fly in amber,
Underneath my rotting burial cloth:

To be called by him. My state was both not-real
And real. For who was I without my knowing?
More like the darkness in its daily fall,
More like the stone, more like the body going,

Collapsing into time. There was the nothing
That I lay in, and only since have I recalled
What must have been—my release to death, the mouthing
Of sorrow as I was mourned. When I was pulled

Back from that other place, I knew I *was*.
I heard him call my name, and then I rose.

Jesus

I am the resurrection, and the life,
And Lazarus is proof. For sometimes faith
Is not enough. God understands their grief,
And knows the greatest human wish is breath

Returned. My God who is in the firmament
Is made of clouds and of Himself, each hue
And every one. I am His instrument,
Who unwraps truth from daily life, to show

Doubt for what it is, and leaves instead
A miracle. *I am the resurrection,*
And the life. Lazarus shows what I have said.
I take him with the firmness of conviction,

And he steps out into the light, removes
His cloth, and through the Word of God, he lives.

Lazarus

Later, it was difficult for me,
For how do you explain to anyone
The line that stands between mortality
And death? At night, sometimes, as I drank wine,

I'd sit in silence, dreaming myself back
To nothing, and, after a while, I could do it,
Become the cave I lay in, and, with luck,
Sometimes, I could go further, when I knew it

Again. For just a moment I would float
Within the darkness made of birth and death.
When morning came, I'd tremble when I ate,
But then the world came back, and I could breathe.

I knew inside the body was the soul,
That stillness in the middle of it all.

Jesus

I thought of him when I was hanging here:
The sweat and blood had fallen in my eyes;
The nails and Romans pierced me everywhere.
I waited for the metamorphosis.

My God, my God, why hast thou forsaken me?
Dangling on a cross between two thieves,
I wondered why I'd walked upon the sea,
Multiplied His fishes and His loaves,

Only to die like this. Why not save *me*?
And, as I died, I was completely human.
I understood the workings of the body
For the first time. That's why I was born of woman:

To be born, to live, to die as every man.
And, afterwards, there was the resurrection.

Lazarus

Later, when death came, I had no fear.
I'd been the walking miracle, the man
Who died and walked again. My life was far
From easy. Who would lie with me? What woman

Yearned to be with death? I knew what kings,
And seers, poets and believers know:
A loneliness, an apartness from all things
And yet connection that other people grow

To yearn for when the other parts of life
Are not enough. I was not frightened then.
It was the elimination of all strife;
It was the natural pathway of all men.

Take me, I said, and after it was done,
I blended who-I-was with earth and stone.

Jesus

Because I was a man, I had some doubt.
Because I was His son, I rose again.
Because I was a man, I had been caught.
Because I was His son, I had the sin

Of the world upon my shoulders. It was hard.
These are the words that I spake unto you.
I was made to suffer and to be the Word
Of God. I am myself but made anew,

The living promise of the life beyond.
We are not stones or trees or dust or water.
We do not have beginning or an end,
Except on earth. Trust that there is something better.

You'll rise again. I know what you've been through.
I suffered human life: and so do you.

ABOUT THE AUTHOR

Kim Bridgford is the director of the West Chester University Poetry Center and the West Chester University Poetry Conference, the largest all-poetry writing conference in the United States. As editor of *Mezzo Cammin*, she was the founder of The *Mezzo Cammin* Women Poets Timeline Project, which was launched at the National Museum of Women in the Arts in Washington on March 27, 2010, and will eventually be the largest database of women poets in the world. She is the author of seven books of poetry: *Undone* (David Robert Books); *Instead of Maps* (David Robert Books); *In the Extreme: Sonnets about World Records* (Story Line Press), winner of the Donald Justice Prize; *Take-Out: Sonnets about Fortune Cookies* (David Robert Books); *Hitchcock's Coffin: Sonnets about Classic Films* (David Robert Books); *Bully Pulpit* (White Violet Press); and *Epiphanies* (David Robert Books). Her work has been nominated for the Pulitzer Prize, the Poets' Prize, and seven times for a Pushcart Prize.

During her tenure at Fairfield University, she became known as one of the best writing program directors in the United States, a teacher of national reputation (a former Connecticut Professor of the Year and a two-time nominee for U.S. Professor of the Year), and one of the best contemporary practitioners of the sonnet. She was the 2007 Connecticut Touring Poet, a series that has included Robert Pinsky, X. J. Kennedy, James Merrill, and Donald Justice.

Her collaborative work with visual artist Jo Yarrington on Iceland, Venezuela, and Bhutan has been honored by a Ucross residency, and has appeared in exhibitions, at conferences, and in journals such as *The Iowa Review, Connecticut Review, The Lyric,* and *The Robert Frost Review.*

Her collaborative work with the Printmakers' Network of Southern New England and poets Sue Standing and Vivian Shipley—the three-book set entitled *Travel*—has been featured at Fairfield University, Wheaton College, the University of Connecticut, and many other venues.

Bridgford has received grants from the National Endowment for the Arts and the Connecticut Commission on the Arts. Her work has appeared on *The Writer's Almanac* with Garrison Keillor, five times on *Verse Daily,* and has been honored by the Catholic Press Association of the United States and Canada. She has appeared in *The New York Times, The Washington Post, The*

Philadelphia Inquirer, The Chronicle of Higher Education, and *The Connecticut Post;* on NPR and the website of *The News Hour with Jim Lehrer;* and in various headline news outlets.

She wrote the introduction to Russell Goings' *The Children of Children Keep Coming,* an epic griot song, and joined Goings in ringing the closing bell of the New York Stock Exchange when the book was released, a week before the first Obama inauguration.